TELL ME A STORY

TELL ME A STORY

Stories for Your Grandchildren and the Art of Telling Them

By Charlie and Martha Shedd

Photographs by Robert A. Lisak

Doubleday & Company, Inc., Garden City, New York   1984

Illustrations by Tony Chen on pages 87, 88, 91, and 94 are
from *The Doubleday Illustrated Children's Bible* by Sandol Stoddard.
Copyright © 1983 by Nelson Doubleday, Inc.
Reproduced by permission of Doubleday and Company, Inc.

"Abou Ben Adhem" on page 106 is
from Burton Egbert Stevenson's *The Home Book of Verse*
(New York: Henry Holt and Company, 1915).

Photographs on pages 30, 134, and 135 are by Sven Marsten.

Library of Congress Cataloging in Publication Data

Shedd, Charlie W.
  Tell me a story.

  Summary: Stories, poems, Bible stories, proverbs, and
other literary selections, chosen to bring the genera-
tions closer together.
    1. Children's literature. [1. Literature—Collections]
I. Shedd, Martha.   II. Lisak, Robert, ill.   III. Title.
PZ5.S516Te   1984   [Fic]
ISBN 0-385-19004-2
83-45568
Text copyright © 1984 by Charlie and Martha Shedd and The Abundance Foundation
Photographs copyright © 1984 by Robert A. Lisak

Contents

PREFACE *"Grandparents Are for Wondering with You"* 9

I HOW TO TELL A STORY—AND HOW NOT TO 11

II TELL ME A STORY 19

CHAPTER ONE *"Once Upon a Time"* 21

The First Jack-o'-Lantern 22

The Burning Cottage 25

Desert Pete 27

She Cut the Ham at Both Ends 28

Circus 31

Better Soap 32

The Jay and the Peacock 34

"S.T." 36

The Wild Duck 37

Who's Important? 39

The Pearl 41

The Bedtime Prayer 42

Chop a Little Wood for the Next Fellow 45

CHAPTER TWO *Stories from Our Own Lives* 47

Where Is This Bus Going? 49

The Three Lost Gloves 51

"A Small Bouquet . . . This Very Day" 52

ESP—or a Divine Voice? 55

Jasper 59

Contents

	The Sheep and the Roses	60
	Start with the Ring	63
	The Christmas Plant	64
	Mr. Midkiff's Flower Garden	65
	Write Your Own Story	68
CHAPTER THREE *Nature*		73
	Love Dance of the Fiddler Crab	76
	The Flying Squirrels	77
	Turtle Tears	79
	The Pacific Golden Plover	83
	The Wounded Egret	84
CHAPTER FOUR *Bible Stories*		86
	David and Goliath—Be Yourself	88
	"I Will Water Your Camels, Too"	90
	Five Loaves and Two Small Fishes	93
	The Prodigal Son	95
CHAPTER FIVE *Poems*		99
	The Falling Apples	101
	The Blacksmith	102
	Just the Place for Us	105
	You, Too?	105
	Abou Ben Adhem	106
	The Blind Men and the Elephant	107
CHAPTER SIX *When Time Is Short*		110
	Choice	110
	Never	111
	Directions	112
	The Two Buckets	112
	The Worst Curse	114
	Indian Chief	114
	Cycling	115
	Needing Special Prayer	115

Contents

CHAPTER SEVEN *Proverbs*   116

       "A Bird in Hand"   118

CHAPTER EIGHT *Epitaphs*   121

III ON MAKING TIME FOR STORYTELLING   125

IV PRAYER OF THE TALKATIVE GRANDPARENT   139

 *PREFACE*

"Grandparents Are for Wondering with You"

"What is a grandparent for?"

"For going to visit on Sunday . . . during Thanksgiving vacation and Christmas . . . in the summer . . . after school . . . when your parents are too busy and you need somebody to be with. . . . Grandparents are for building you toys . . . for making nut bread . . . for answering your questions . . . for taking care of you if your mother is sick . . . for playing games together . . . for telling you stories when you go to bed . . . for making you laugh . . . for really listening when you need to talk about things. . . . Grandparents are for wondering with you."

Straight from the grandchild front come all these answers. Ask any group of grandchildren, "What is a grandparent for?" and here they come: pensive, provocative, deep, challenging answers to make us think, "What *are* we for?"

In a quieter day with slower pace, mothers and fathers might have taken more time for parenting. But in today's fast world too many important things are pushed aside. One of these could be family togetherness, and what an opening for us! If grandpa and grandma can step in now with the right amount of input at the right time, this may be our verse: "Surely thou art come to the kingdom for such a time as this." We may be exactly what the grandchild needs for strength and character in the years to come. As one grandchild put it, "The thing I like so much about my grandparents is how they will say, 'What do *you* think?'"

The magic phrase for storytelling:
WHAT DO YOU THINK?

And the second is like unto it:
TELL ME MORE.

I

HOW TO TELL A STORY—AND HOW NOT TO

Every child loves a story. No exception, at least not at the beginning. Innate in the grandchild's makeup is this wonderful fact: From the Maker of children, grandchildren come ready for grandpa and grandma stories. Right subject, right length, right spirit, "Tell me a story" may represent more than a nice invitation. Couldn't this even be the moment for molding a bit of tomorrow?

How does a child develop character, reach conclusions, learn good judgment, sort truth from trivia, accept, reject, establish values, build fiber? No one knows all the ways of shaping quality citizens, but this we have clearly seen: *Somewhere in the background of the quality young there was quality love.* From where did it come? Parents, teacher, friend, neighbor? From all, from one. Somebody was giving these young people time, helping them think, listening, wondering with them. And this too we know for sure, because we've seen it often—sometimes the love which made them strong was grandparent love.

Isn't it awesome that we by such a simple thing as storytelling could be fortifying the future? In this light we come to the question, "What kind of stories will grandchildren listen to?"

From speaking often in the youth scene, sharing thoughts in dialogue, and from storytelling time with our own grandchildren, we have drawn up some how-to's and how-not-to's. These are for us, because we need them. Most of us grandparents have in us this ever so human tendency to overdo on the input. Having lived long, experienced much, learned our lessons, we have so many answers. Why shouldn't we tell it like it is? To which question there is only one answer. We shouldn't because, no matter how interesting we are, every person we meet has a "self" more interesting than our "self."

This we must never forget when we come bringing stories. No matter what we say, in the heart of our listener that major echo sounds "Me," "My," "I," "Mine" (and sometimes "Ours").

How to Tell Our Grandpa/Grandma Stories

Say it again and never forget this is number one, always number one—
Number one: Grandchildren love stories about themselves.
"Let me tell you about the day you were born."

"Remember that time you fell in the lake?"

"Did you know that when you were four years old you already knew the alphabet?"

On and on almost forever, these happenings out of their own lives are number one.

Number two: Grandchildren love stories made to order for their uniqueness. Because each grandchild is an individual, the stories focusing on their special interests, their special qualities, can almost never fail.

Number three: Grandchildren like stories about their heritage. Uncles, aunts, cousins, close relatives, plus those from the distant past—these also have a special appeal.

Number four: Grandchildren like stories about *us* if we don't overdo. Interesting bits of this and that from grandpa/grandma backgrounds will be appreciated to a point. And always that point points to this point: "The point is, grandpa and grandma, how does this affect *me?*"

We call these first how-to's the flashback stories, and that word "flash" is all important. Almost without exception the best grandparent storytellers we know have learned this truth: Memory road, if we are to keep it interesting, must be constantly flashing to this day and tomorrow and the days beyond that. Always for our grandchildren the past is but *prologue* to the future. And always a number-one killer of grandparent-grandchild rapport is "Back in the good old days."

So "These our roots and this our history" can be a good focus. Yet forever the emphasis must be "The best song hasn't been sung yet, the best poem hasn't been rhymed."

Then isn't there one more reason grandchildren enjoy the flashback stories? Rightly introduced, rightly told, and rightly terminated, haven't they also made another contribution to solid character? This is the stabilizing sensation, "Here I belong!"

Before we move to the how-not-to's, here are three more types for our "like" list:

Number five: Grandchildren like stories about other grandchildren.

Number six: Grandchildren like humorous stories.

Number seven: Grandchildren like stories with subtle meanings; stories they can turn over again and again; stories which extend them the dignity of using their own minds. Which leads to our first how-not-to:

The How-Not-To's

As everyone knows, "Stop" signs along the way are equally as important as the "Go" signals. Because this is true, the skilled grandparent storyteller will avoid some more certain turnoffs.

Number one: We will do our very best to *avoid "talking down."* And could anyone improve on this for positive commentary to our first negative? (It's from a university senior, psychology major.)

One thing I remember about my grandparents is how they would sit on the floor and talk with me. Why do I always think of that when I think of them? Do you suppose it is because almost always adults talk down to children? I mean they do physically, sure, and part of that is nothing but size. Yet if you study this, you'll see what I mean. They "talk down" in other ways too.

Number two: Because this is another number-one killer of a grandchild's interest, we will also *avoid the "preachy."* Threats, warnings, condemnations: all taboo. So should everything be positive? Isn't the message "no" sometimes? Should we dismiss the judgment factor always? To which the answer: The oh, so delicate secret is to only provide some judgment roads. Gates, doors, avenues, paths we may lead them to but, having done that, we go away. Down these roads they must find their own "no's!"

Why is it so hard to put aside the preachy? Probably because in the early years "no" was an absolute must. Children without fences become confused, plus dangerous. But blessed is the family where parents have learned (grandparents too) at the right moment to say, "Here you must go it alone."

Number three: So talking down is "avoid" number one and forever close behind is "preachy." But there is one more deadly tendency we must avoid. We must *avoid the interminable.*

We've referred previously to this "avoid" and for us at least we'll say it again and again—it's an ugly word, "interminable."

> *She was a bore. Much to my sorrow,*
> *She was here today and here tomorrow!*

Haven't all of us known a few "she's" like that? Plus some of the masculine gender. And woe to the grandpa or grandma of whom it could be said, "Interminable."

Stories too long, stories overdetailed, stories with too many dull spots turn off the listener in all of us.

Now on to stories from our collection. These stories we've told our own grandchildren. Stories from the past, personal stories, stories long, stories short, stories for wondering.

Stories which for us go best when we remember the two magic phrases:

WHAT DO *YOU* THINK?
TELL ME MORE.

II

TELL ME
A STORY

CHAPTER ONE

"Once Upon a Time"

A few favorite stories from two grandparents who, like all good grandparents, pray this special prayer:

> *Lord, may we be builders of bridges;*
>   *bridges whereby old truths*
>   *pass over for new influence;*
>   *new influence on some very special*
>   *new people,*
>   *our grandchildren.*

The First Jack-o'-Lantern

Have you heard the story of the first jack-o'-lantern?

Once upon a time when our country belonged to the Indians, they tried to frighten the early settlers away.

In a certain settlement two little pioneer sisters were left home alone one day. Their mother and father had gone to the village to sell corn.

That day the girls brought in some pumpkins from the garden to scrape out the insides for making pumpkin pies. That day, too, the parents were delayed and, wouldn't you know, this was the day some Indians came in from the forest. Out there at the edge of their woods the sisters saw their visitors, and they also saw that the Indians didn't go away. It was getting dark now and they were afraid. What could they do?

Somewhere the sisters had learned that Indians had a natural fear of "evil spirits." So they had a great idea. They would cut eyes, nose, and a big grinning mouth in a pumpkin shell. Then they would put a candle in the pumpkin and place it in their window.

You can imagine, when the Indians saw the big yellow face, this was too much. Those flaming eyes, the nose, the mouth; they had never seen such a thing. This must be *the* real evil spirit. So they ran back to the forest.

That is how jack-o'-lanterns came to be.

Have you ever seen these words, "Don't panic!"? Let's talk about that.

The Burning Cottage

Once upon a time, long, long ago, there was a small fishing village where the people needed one more catch. One more catch would see them through the winter, but without this catch they might be short of food.

It was the season of rough water now and the wives did not want their men to go. Still, they went.

Then, exactly as the women feared, came a storm. This was a mighty storm, one of the worst. How could their husbands make it home through these high waves, through the wind and darkness?

At last the frightened wives met at the dock to pray. Then, as they were praying, they heard a sound; and when they looked up, high on the hill they saw a cottage burning. Of course they ran at once to see what they could do, but they were too late.

How did it happen? Why? And then came the answer. Annie, one of the newer brides, was crying. She knew why it happened. She had forgotten to blow out her candles. So they gathered to comfort her when suddenly there was a shout.

"Look! The boats! Our men have made it safely home."

Laughing and shouting, they ran to meet their husbands. Happiness everywhere, with this one exception. Annie was so sad and as she made her report to Eric, she sobbed, "How will you ever forgive me?" Whereupon the big fisherman put his arm around his little bride and said, "Annie, you must not cry. It was the light from our burning cottage that brought us safely home."

Time for wondering together:
Is there any happening in your life, our lives, when something ever so bad turned into something ever so good?

Desert Pete

It's an old story, told many times, but this version will do for us.

You are very thirsty, thirstier than you've ever been. You've been walking across the desert, and you are so tired, so hot. But worst of all, you're thirstier than you've ever been.

Suddenly you come over a little knoll and there on the other side is a pump. It's a rusty old pump set on a rickety platform. On its handle hangs a tin cup and, tied fast to the tin cup is a note.

Naturally you unfasten the note, and this is the message:

> This pump'll draw water if you go at it right. Over there under the rock is a bottle of water. If you'll pour the water into the top of the pump, and then pump like crazy, I promise you'll get all the water you can drink, and it's good cool water.
>
> I know the pump works. I fixed its washers last week. I also know you'll want to drink a little from the bottle, but I'm warning you, if you do, that's all the water you'll get. It will take the whole bottle to prime the pump. If you do what I tell you, you'll see. Good luck.
>
> > Signed
> > *Desert Pete*

> P.S. When you've had all the water you can hold, fill the bottle, and put it under the rock for the next fellow.

What would you *do?*

She Cut the Ham at Both Ends

Once upon a time a young husband went out to buy a ham. This was soon after the honeymoon and they were about to share their first ham dinner. He liked the way she cooked it, but as they sat down for dinner he noticed something different. She had cut both ends from the ham and why would she do that?

When he asked her why, she answered, "My mother always cut off both ends before she cooked a ham."

Then, when he checked with her mother, he learned another interesting thing. Her mother didn't have an answer either except that her mother had always cut off both ends of a ham.

Fortunately for the curious husband, Grandma was living too and at last came the chance to question her. "I have been wondering something, Grandma, why do you cut off both ends of a ham?"

"Oh," she said, "that's easy. My pans are all too small for a whole ham."

What funny thing do we do because of our childhood programming?

Circus

Once upon a time there was a country boy who went to his first circus. On circus day the boy's father gave him a silver dollar and told him he could ride his pony nine miles to the county seat for the big show.

It was noon when the boy arrived, and the streets were crowded with happy people. He tied his pony to a hitching post and ran to the main street where something wonderful was happening. Excitement filled the air.

Pushing his way through the crowd, the boy found himself staring at a sight such as he had never seen. There before him, down the street came the circus. Camels, horses, ponies, acrobats, elephants, zebras, brass bands, and wagon after wagon with wild animals. The boy's eyes filled with wonder and amazement. At last he was actually seeing a circus.

As the boy stood there, the clowns came walking at the rear of the procession. One of them, with his hand held out, seemed to be coming toward the boy. So, as the big clown passed, the boy reached into his pocket for his silver dollar and, quick as a flash, dropped it in the waiting hand.

The big clown bowed in regal splendor and walked on.

Minutes later, after the crowd had melted away, the boy went back to his pony and rode home. It was not until some time later that he discovered the awful truth. He hadn't seen the circus at all. What he saw was only the parade.

What do you *think?*

Better Soap

An ambitious yet discouraged young man called on a successful businessman. He came to ask him the secret of success.

"No secret at all," replied the businessman. "Whatever you do, do well. Then keep doing it better and better."

"But," said the young man, "there isn't anything I can do."

"A wise thinker," said the businessman, "told me, 'Every man born into the world has his work born with him.' So you must have something you can do. What are you doing now?"

Not very proud of his work, the young man answered, "All I can do is make soap."

"Go home," answered the businessman, "go home and make a better soap today than you have ever made before. Then tomorrow improve on that."

The young man followed the businessman's advice. He decided to get out of his ruts, to make different kinds of bars, different shapes, different sizes. Then he added a scent to the soap. This really was something new. So on and on he improved his product until at last his soaps became the favorites of a buying public.

Today there is almost no one in any part of the civilized world who hasn't heard his name. That young man who had considered himself a colossal failure was William Colgate.

Next time you use Colgate toothpaste, Palmolive soap, or any number of Colgate-Palmolive products, you can say, "Hmm! If all the people in the world do have their work born with them, maybe we should talk about mine."

The Jay and the Peacock

Once upon a time there was a man named Aesop. He was famous for his fables. Fable means "small story with big lesson." One of Aesop's fables° is the story of "The Jay and the Peacock."

There was a jay who was never quite satisfied being a jay and especially he wasn't satisfied when he had seen the peacocks. Why couldn't *he* have long feathers and flashy colors too? So every day he went to see the peacocks.

If only he could be like that! If only!

Then one day, while he was watching, he had a great idea. Peacocks have a way of dropping certain feathers and leaving them on the ground. This is called molting. Why couldn't he take these feathers and put them in his wings and tail? Then wouldn't he look like a peacock?

That is exactly what he did and it was really a very good job of making himself over.

Now he looked enough like the peacocks, he would go and join them. For a time none of the peacocks noticed him. Then one of the scouter peacocks took a second look, and a third. Suddenly he let out a peacock screech and all the peacocks came running. The game was over.

You probably know what happened next. The peacocks pounced on Mr. Jay. Pecking, clawing, they tore off all his feathers. Peacock feathers, jay feathers, all his feathers. So there he was, poor naked bird. Only one thing left for him to do. Humbled and beaten, he went back to the jays.

° Aesop's fables may be found in many libraries. Aesop was a master at making important points and, retold in simple language, even their antiquated phraseology is easily understood. Most children have never heard of Aesop, which leads to another plus: Today's precocious young, proud of their minds, take well to old things properly presented.

I almost hate to tell you what happened next. Since he didn't look like a jay either now, they too pounced on him and drove him away.

Aesop concluded each of his fables with the single word, "Moral."

What do you think the moral might be from "The Jay and the Peacock"?

"S.T."

Once upon a time two brothers were convicted of stealing sheep. By the strange custom of that faraway land, they were branded on their foreheads with the two letters "S" and "T," meaning "Sheep Thief."

Reuben, unable to bear the shame, ran away. But wherever he fled, men asked after the two strange letters, so he kept wandering. Restless, hopelessly miserable, full of bitterness, at length he took his own life.

Thomas, on the other hand, said to himself, "I can't run away from the fact that I stole sheep. I'll face it. I will stay here and win back my self-respect, plus the respect of those around me."

Years passed and by his good deeds Thomas built for himself a reputation. "Here," the people said, "is a man of integrity. A man to be honored. Finest man in many valleys."

To a ripe old age Thomas lived, and the longer he lived the more he dedicated his life to good deeds and the blessing of people. At last he died and so loved was he that people came from miles around to the little church to pay their respects at his last rites.

If you had been there, they say you would have heard this strange exchange of words at his coffin. A newcomer to the village said to one of the men of affairs, "I haven't known him long, but I have often wondered what mean these letters 'S.T.' on his forehead?"

"Aye," replied the merchant, "I have forgotten the particulars, but I believe they mean 'Saint Thomas.'"

What do you *think?*

The Wild Duck

Once there was a duck, as fine a duck as ever you did see. And being a wild duck, every fall he flew south with the other ducks. Then every spring he came north again with the rest of his flock.

One summer there was a drought and corn was hard to find. Ducks grow hungry when food is scarce and this one was very hungry. Then on a certain day he and his friends were flying over a barnyard when he noticed the farmer scattering corn for the chickens. Beautiful golden kernels of corn. So said he, "I will drop down and join the domestics. Then after dinner, with an extra burst of speed, I'll catch up with my flying friends."

The corn was delicious, but when he had filled himself he felt so comfortable, so rested, he decided to stay overnight. That evening, feeling quite at home, he entered the coop to enjoy the warmth of the brooder house.

"In the morning," he thought, "I will double my speed and be back with my flock." So morning came and now, oh, wonderful surprise, more wonderful golden corn. Of course, he ate his fill again and then he remembered his mother said, "Never fly on a full stomach." So he decided to wait till noon, but noontime found him thinking of the corn he could have that evening. Why couldn't he stay over and join another flock on its southern way tomorrow? But tomorrow, same excuses, same feelings, until at last our friend gave up his good intention. Why shouldn't he stay and enjoy what he had? Not a bad life, not at all. The rest of the winter he would sleep warm, eat himself full, round out his figure, loll in comfort.

Finally spring came as it always does and there went the flocks overhead, bound for north country. Now, stirring within Mr. Duck was the call of the wild again. "Good-bye, winter friends," he cried and, flapping his wings, he took off.

But alas, poor butterball friend could mount no higher than the barnyard fence. Too soft, too round, too heavy, he was grounded.

What do you think finally happens to fat ducks?
Tell me more.

Who's Important?

There is a lovely legend which centers about the building of a great cathedral. When the project began, heaven's director of church construction announced a grand contest. On completion of this cathedral, the Lord would award a rare prize to that person who had made the most significant contribution to the finished edifice. It was expected, of course, that there would be no argument, no explanation. The Lord could do no wrong.

Naturally, there was considerable speculation. Who would be the favored winner? The architect? That was a prime possibility. Maybe the contractor? One of the craftsmen who did rare work in glass, gold, iron, brass? Could it be the sculptor? Perhaps the stonemason? Maybe the carpenter assigned to that intricate grill above the altar?

Throughout the building of the cathedral, each did his best, and the result was such a masterpiece as had never been seen in all the land.

But at the moment of high anticipation when the winner was announced, imagine: The recipient proved to be an old peasant woman who had daily carried fodder to the ox that pulled the marble for the masons.*

Now what could a story like that be saying to us?

* Charlie Shedd, *Time for All Things* (Nashville, Tenn.: Abingdon Press, 1962), p. 88.

The Pearl

John Steinbeck was a famous American author and one of his most famous stories was "The Pearl."

Kino was a simple pearl diver. He lived with his wife, Juana, and their little son, Coyotito, in the village of pearl divers. All the divers were equally poor, barely making a living by their labors.

Then one day Kino brought up a magnificent pearl. It was larger and more nearly perfect than any pearl the villagers had ever seen. For Kino and his family this meant wealth beyond their wildest dreams. It meant a rifle for Kino, a better house for Juana, education for little Coyotito.

Yet, unfortunately, that isn't all it meant. It meant jealousy in the hearts of the villagers. Where before there had been only friendship, now there was envy. It meant the greed of pearl merchants, too, who clamored to buy the pearl. It meant fear that someone might steal from Kino. Jealousy, greed, ill feeling, fear—these were things Kino had never known. And worst of all, he was forced to admit a hardness coming in his own heart, a hardness he would never have believed.

At last, in desperation, Kino stood one day on the beach and threw his perfect pearl as far out into the sea as he could possibly throw it.

Why would he do a thing like that?

The Bedtime Prayer

Once upon a time a small boy named Donny knelt beside his grandmother's knee to pray.

"Now I lay me down to sleep," he began. "I pray thee, Lord, my soul to keep. If I should die before I wake . . ." Then he said it again: "If I should die before I wake."

"Wait a minute," he called as he ran downstairs. But in a few moments he was back and, kneeling once more, he finished his prayer.

You can imagine his grandmother simply had to ask why the interruption. And this is what Donny said. "Well, this afternoon Teddy"—his little brother—"took my football. That made me mad at him and, just to get even, I went into his room and stood his wooden soldiers on their heads. He gets so-o-o mad when I do that.

"When I came to that part about 'If I should die before I wake,' all of a sudden I thought, 'If I *should* die, I wouldn't want him to find his soldiers that way.'"

Nice going, Donny.

The Bible says:

If you come to the altar and there remember your brother has something against you, go and straighten it out with your brother.

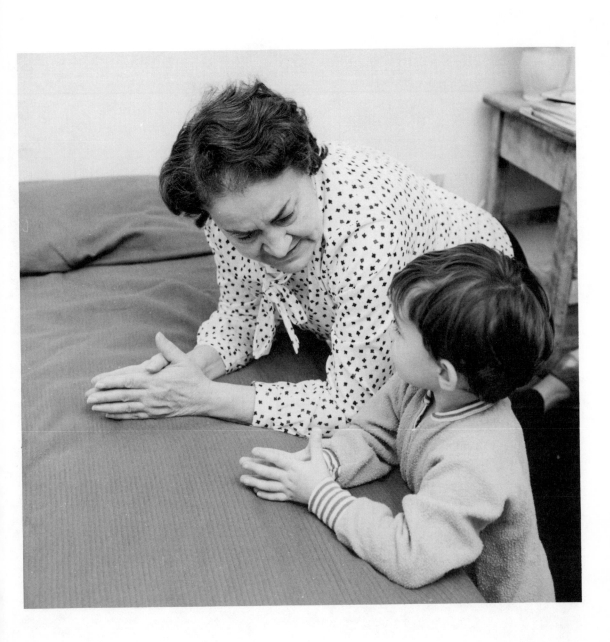

Chop a Little Wood for the Next Fellow

In Ottawa, Canada, they tell the story of three wealthy businessmen who came from their city for a fishing trip. Patrick Monday was the best guide around. He was an old Indian who knew where the fish were and fortunately he was free right then, so they hired him.

After several fine days, when they had caught their limit, they packed and prepared for their return. Early next morning they rose, broke camp, and were ready for departure. But where was Patrick Monday?

When they had called and called but heard no answer, they stilled themselves to listen. Then, with their voices lowered, they heard chopping up at the cabin. There they found Patrick Monday cutting wood.

"But, Pat," they said, "we don't need more wood. Let's go." Whereupon the Indian straightened himself, looked them square in the eye, and said, "Up here it is our custom to chop a little wood for the next fellow."

What do you think?

CHAPTER TWO

Stories from Our Own Lives

"Repeat."
  "Remember."
    "Say it again."
Grandchildren prefer stories in this order:

The stories they like best are stories about themselves.

They also like stories about their family, including us. Rightly told, in right spirit, they do enjoy those grandpa-grandma stories. What kind? Many kinds, but in the words of one grandchild, "Tell me some more stories about when you did some dumb thing." Why do they like to know about our mistakes? Is it because if their favorite people do "some dumb thing" there must be hope for them?

As our grandchildren develop, their preference may shift to stories with more subtle meanings. Now they will appreciate us more if we recognize their growing intelligence and show an increasing respect for their sharp young minds. All these preferences we can build on to create that priceless rapport which knows no generation gap.

When this full rapport is established, grandchildren will even be ready for some of the harder things. As sure as the next heartbeat, our grandchildren will see some difficult times. By adequate forethought and careful picking of moments, by the sharing of our own hard places, couldn't we be getting them ready for their own valleys? Is there any living grandparent who hasn't suffered? Alone or in duet, we've been over some rough roads. Sorrow, losses, pain. These too, unless we moan too long, can be a part of our sharing.

Other coming events in the life of most every grandchild are courtship, love, marriage. Here we may bring a special offering. Math, English, history, sports, music, computers—all these plus many more items new and old are part of today's education. But isn't there still one void? Who's getting them ready for those intricate relationships when the honeymoon is over?

Too many young lovers may be overly euphoric, expecting heaven on earth as they walk down the aisle. Yet we who are the veterans of love know that great marriage is not all moonlight and violins, all candlelight and roses. So wouldn't this be one fine contribution from any grandparent:

"Listen, my children, the greatest love is also shaped by pounding on anvils of sacrifice and compromise. Would you like to think with me about your love life twenty years from now, or forty?"

Properly phrased and again in right spirit, grandchildren will ponder long with us as we discuss their future.

And this we can know as another of the absolutes. In their future they hope for happiness. Ask any group of the young, or any one of them alone, "What do you want from tomorrow?"; always on their answer list are words like "fun," "good times," "enjoy."

Is that bad? No, that's good if it includes this one thing we have learned: Happiness is a by-product. That being true, we as grandparents may be the very ones to lead them toward the more lasting good times.

From a grandmother's letter:
Many people in our world, including my grandchildren's parents (sad to say), are driving so hard for the big blessings, they miss the smaller ones.

If I had to select only one gift for my grandchildren this would be it—I would give them the ability to enjoy their little enjoyments each day, every day, all day.

Where Is This Bus Going?

One day in Chicago we were riding the bus when we were treated to a hundred-yard dash. The early morning commuter scene is a fascinating study in any big city, and this man made one marvelous run for our bus.

We wished afterward we had been timing him, because he must have broken a world's record. Then he made his last spring, landed on the step, peered anxiously into the face of the conductor, and asked:

"Where is this bus going?"

Aren't there some things we should be asking before *the mad dash?*

The Three Lost Gloves

Karen and Richard are among our very good friends. They're a fun couple, and particularly fun because they can laugh at themselves.

This is one of their fun stories.

Richard had lost a glove. Nothing major about losing a glove except what good is one glove when you need two?

"Now," says Karen, "I made a big mistake. I got up on my high and mighty. 'Richard,' I said, 'there is really no excuse for this. If you would do what I do, that couldn't happen. See? I make a habit of putting my gloves inside my hat. Of course, I never forget my hat, so how could I lose my gloves?"

Shortly after he lost that glove, Richard and Karen were on an extended trip. They were sitting now in a laundromat waiting for their clothes to dry. Talking, reading, waiting.

When the job was done and they returned to their motel, Karen panicked. She had left her hat (gloves in it) at the laundromat. Of course they hurried back and this is the bad news. No hat. No gloves. Someone had carried them away.

What would you say if you were Richard?

Karen says, "You aren't going to believe this, but I want you to know Richard never said one word, not one word. Here we were now with one glove for the two of us, and he never said one word."

"A Small Bouquet . . . This Very Day"

When we were attending the University of Chicago, every day we rode the three-ten trolley home. That was a good thing for us, because one day we saw an extra fine example of how to deal with people. Most days on the three-ten trolley there was this old gray-haired motorman who never missed one chance to be nice.

When he passed somebody's get-off corner, he would apologize and even back up if he could. When a mother came aboard with her children, he was never quite content until they were well seated. If a lady boarded with bags and boxes, he would give her a hand. We thought this man was a living personification of what a living Lord would look like running a streetcar.

Every day he was an inspiration. So one day when traffic was light, we told him we liked his style; we introduced ourselves; and from that moment on he always called us by name.

Then we decided to write a letter of praise to the superintendent of Chicago Transit Lines. Nothing special, just a plain word of thanks for one employee. Identification? No problem. There at the front of his car, each conductor had not only his name but his picture and his special number.

Next?

Are you ready for this? Within forty-eight hours we had a letter back from the superintendent, Chicago Transit Lines.

You will never know how much we appreciate your writing us. We have so many complaints, but hardly ever a word of commendation. We have posted your letter on the company bulletin board and you may be sure your conductor will be duly rewarded.

It was the weekend, but on Monday when we boarded the three-ten that dear old conductor stopped his car, took our hands in his, and with eyes a little bit teary said, "I been working this line for twenty-three years and that's the first time anybody ever told me I done a good job."

Is this what the poet meant?

> *'Tis better to buy a small bouquet*
> *And give to someone this very day*
> *Than a bushel of roses, white and red,*
> *To lay on their coffin after they're dead.*

ESP—or a Divine Voice?

"I need to see you right away!"

It was a plaintive voice and obviously the lady was troubled. As she came through my office door, she looked like a normal person. Attractive, young, intelligent. But bothered! And this is the story she told me:

"This morning the strangest thing happened. It was about 2 A.M. when I was suddenly wide awake. I turned on the lights and looked around. There was this loud noise in my ears like a horse neighing."

Then she went on to say that she owned two horses, but they were in a pasture five miles from her apartment. Since she had always wanted a horse, now that she was earning a good salary, she had bought two horses of her very own. Riding was her big hobby and she had a special feeling for her horses.

When the sound died, she turned off her lights and settled back. But in a few minutes there it was again. Same sound, a bit more intense now. This time she sat up in bed, cleared her head, and waited. Then once more the sound came, louder, clearer.

Of course she thought of her own horses, and then she felt an urge to go see them. "How silly can I be?" she asked herself. "Are you losing your mind? It's two o'clock in the morning!"

Yet inside she still felt this strong urge. So she dressed, called the night guard to bring her car, and off she drove down the freeway.

"Please don't laugh," she went on. "When I arrived, there in the glow of my flashlight my palomino mare was standing in broken wire neighing her lungs out."

Some horses are like that. They seem to sense that the wise thing right now is, "Don't move. Call for help."

So the horse stood still while her mistress untangled the barbed wire and set her free with nothing more than minor scratches.

"What do you think happened?" she went on in her lovely Texas drawl. "I couldn't possibly have heard with my ears through the night sounds and the hum of the freeway. So many noises in a big city like this!"

When I described all this to our family at the dinner table that night, Peter said something we've never forgotten. Peter was twelve and children do have a way of putting things in a nutshell, don't they?

I asked, "What do *you* think?" Quiet for a time, then Peter said, "I think either the lady is lying or God told her to go see about her horse."

What do you *think?*

Certain stories will invariably bring certain surface answers. Example: Whenever we deal with the hard-to-explain, one deduction sure to follow is, "Oh, that's ESP," or "In school we learned about electromagnetic waves. Maybe that's what happened."

But for those of us with beliefs to share, isn't this also the time for probing deeper? "Who do you think is behind the ESP? Who made the electromagnetic waves? Did God tell her to go see about her horse?"

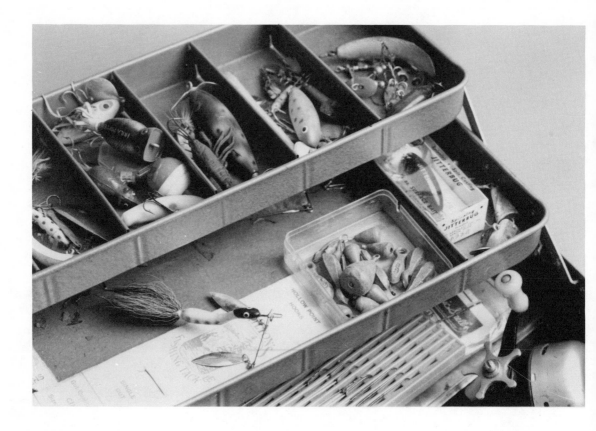

Jasper

Jasper had retired early. He was one of two owners in a hotel chain, and this is his story. He told it to me so often out there fishing in his boat, I can give it to you almost word for word.

"Five years ago my partner came up with an expansion plan. Sure, it would cost something, but without too much risk we could double the number of our hotels. 'Jasper,' he would say, 'over the next ten years we'll make a million.' I like that. I like to make money. But I also like to fish. I like the ocean, nature, the world around me. Then I'd always wanted a garden, and I wanted to raise birds. Quail, pheasant, partridge, all kinds of game birds.

"Well, the more I thought, the more I decided I'd say no. If I sold out to him, I'd have all I needed to do all these things right now.

"You can believe my partner didn't like it. What he said was, 'Jasper, you've lost your mind. Stay with me. We'll make it big.'

"You know what? He made his million, probably more. Didn't even take him ten years. Then one day poor guy had one massive heart attack and died.

"Me? I'm still fishing."

What do you think?

The Sheep and the Roses

We have a friend in Colorado who raises sheep, thousands of sheep. And through the years she's become an expert on grazing, feeding, breeding, shearing, lambing, everything connected with sheep.

Have you ever been to a place where they were raising great numbers of sheep? On the hills and in the pastures you might never notice the smell. But in the lambing pens, the shearing stalls, the breeding places, you'd notice for sure. It wouldn't be any time till you'd be saying, "Isn't that awful? How could anyone stand it every day, year after year?"

One way our friend stands it is *roses*, all kinds of roses. In fact, she has so many roses, she's an expert also on roses.

In front of her house and on both sides she has arranged an absolutely gorgeous display of roses. And if you could stand there admiring, you would sense the care she's given her roses. Planting, pruning, blending of colors, beautiful. Of course, there is one other thing: She has an endless supply of the very finest fertilizer.

One day when we were exclaiming on the splendor, our friend picked a rose and asked, "Don't you especially like the smell of this one?" We did, but it was her next statement we've never forgotten. Maybe one reason we've never forgotten is that we need to think of it often. We need it with people and happenings and all kinds of things.

This is what the lady said:

"When I first started raising sheep, that's all I could smell, just sheep. But then I decided I couldn't settle for that. So now I have my roses to tend and look at, and mostly to smell. Do you know, after a while, I taught myself to smell the roses in spite of the sheep."

Questions for grandchildren:
On a scale of 0 to 10 what grade do I give myself for:
  1. My ability to manage things I don't like _____
  2. My ingenuity at superimposing something positive on the
    negatives _____

Questions for grandparents:
Can my grandchildren understand such words as "ingenuity" and "superimposing"?
ANSWER: That depends on the grandchild. But doesn't it also depend on another thing? This is our ability to present, and explain, and help.

And straight from the grandchild front comes now this loaded observation: "One thing I like about my grandmother is how sometimes she will talk to me like I am a grown-up."

Start with the Ring

When I was seven my father gave me a puzzle. I had the mumps right then, and I needed something to occupy my time.

It was a wooden puzzle shaped like a ball. Numerous pieces. Interesting designs. Various sizes.

I knew it wasn't impossible, because it came all put together, and in its original shape it was very attractive. But, taken apart, it was very confusing. Challenging, yes; exciting, yes; but confusing!

For many hours I gave it my all. This way. That way. Every way. And then at last I decided there was no way. So I put the puzzle in its box, every last piece of it, and called my sister. Would she please take this horrible thing and remove it far, far away. Take it to school. Take it to the trash. Take it anywhere out of my sight forever.

But you know how these things do when you finally give up? They don't give up on you. Next day, there it was in my head again. And my sister, God bless her chubby little intuition, had picked up on that possibility. Instead of discarding it as per instructions, she'd taken it to her room. Somehow she sensed her chubby brother might go for one more try—or another whole day of trying.

Thank you, Mary Frances! That day, that very day, I discovered the secret. Big surprise. You start at the center, see, and go from there. Right here at the center, look. These two wooden rings. Slip these over the main peg and everything fits together. Beautiful. Like a wonderful serendipity.

What things in my life today only fit right one way?

The Christmas Plant

One year at Christmas we were given a strange gift. It came from two of our best friends. But it looked like more of a put-on than a gift.

When we opened the box, there carefully wrapped was a dried-up plant. Brown and brittle leaves, gray stems, dirt on the bulb. What could it be?

The company which sold it to our friends must have known how it would appear at first sight. So they included this card with the words:

Please don't throw me away. I really am a beautiful "Star of Bethlehem" plant. Put me in a dark place, water me, and wait.

We did. And some time later came the miracle. Then the direction slip said, "When it begins to get green, bring it into the light. You will be surprised!"

And we were!

What looked so dead came alive now with green, blue, white, red, touches of gold, deep yellow. Fascinating! Away at the center all that time a dormant beauty had been stirring.

Let's talk about, "Was there ever anything I thought was finished that wasn't?"

Mr. Midkiff's Flower Garden

In one little town where we lived, there was an unusual crippled man. His name was Mr. Midkiff and he tended the railroad crossing.

This was a train-switching town. Like most railroad towns, it was not very attractive. In train-switching towns the dull gray of smoke, soot, and dirt finally takes over.

But there was another reason why our town wasn't much for looks. Back in horse-and-buggy days, the old-timers said, things had been different. Now many doors were locked, windows boarded over, shutters falling, because almost everyone had given up. We were too close to a city. Since these were no longer horse-and-buggy days, off we went to the larger shopping centers.

Mr. Midkiff's job was to sit up there in the observation tower and get ready for the trains. When he knew a train was coming, he would lower the crossing bars. Then he would come down his ladder, hold up his STOP sign, and blow his whistle. Do you know why they had both crossing bars and a man to blow his whistle? It was because boys and girls coming from school might try to slip through the bars and beat the train.

It really wasn't much of a job, but it was probably all Mr. Midkiff could handle. He had been injured years before when he was working for the Union Pacific Railroad. I often heard him say, "Lucky I wasn't killed. Real lucky."

So now they had him doing what he could do, and most of the time it was a dull life for Mr. Midkiff. Even with several trains daily, it was still dull.

What could he do to counteract the boredom?

One day years before we knew him, Mr. Midkiff had an answer. In all that spare time between trains, he could plant a garden, a garden of flowers right there beside the tracks. Zinnias, asters, poppies, roses, flowers of every kind to keep his garden blooming. Something blooming at least a little every season, and from the spring to winter, lavish blooms, every color.

Did you ever live where you had to wait for trains? Often? Aggravating, isn't it? And isn't it uncanny how many times you have to wait when you're in a hurry, or late for an appointment, or going somewhere fun?

Yet what else could we do? We could fuss, scold, pout, wish we lived somewhere else. Or we had one other option. We could admire the flowers.

Then there was another thing we could do. If this was a passenger train, we could watch the passengers as they caught sight of the flowers.

If you've ridden the train much, you know that most stops and much of the slow going seems to be in the ugliest settings. Dirt, smoke, soot, dull gray again. So if you could see flowers right then, you would be especially glad.

That became another interesting thing as we sat at the crossing. To see the passengers looking, smiling, exclaiming!! Here in this shabby little town on a gloomy day, an ever so welcome touch, a bit of beauty.

How well do we accept circumstances we don't like; things we wouldn't have chosen for ourselves; the unexciting parts of life?

What is my grade for taking the ordinary and making it better?

Write Your Own Story

Always, no exception, one hundred percent of the time things which have happened to us have a flavor all their own. A double flavor? The flavor of excitement which comes from recalling happenings out of our personal background. Plus, the opening of our hearts and lives a bit to grandchildren who may always have warm recall because we told them these things right out of our own lives. That's why we are leaving the following pages for *you* to write in, creating your own gift of love and memory for your grandchildren.

_____

_____

_____

_____

_____

_____

_____

_____

_____

_____

_____

_____

_____

_____

_____

_____

_____

_____

_____

_____

_____

_____

_____

_____

_____

_____

CHAPTER THREE

Nature

Doth not nature itself teach us?
I Corinthians 11:14

The world around us is alive with magnificent material for grandparent story-telling. Those of us who are nature lovers have an inexhaustible library of resource material for sharing with the small, the growing, and even with adult grandchildren.

O Lord, our Lord, how manifold are Thy works.
  In wisdom hast Thou made them all.
I want to be an alert grandparent.
  Alert to the wonders of Your world;
  and alert for every opportunity to pass them on.

Amen.

Love Dance of the Fiddler Crab

The fiddler crab is a most unusual creature. A male fiddler crab looks like a violinist. One of his front claws is large, the other small. And when he runs (very fast) he goes sideways. Yet there are few of nature's small beings more expert at communication than the fiddler crab. And especially in speaking the language of love, this little creature is the expert.

At low tide a male fiddler runs along the sandy beach. When he meets a female, he raises his big claw and waves to her. If she responds and comes closer, he puts the full force of his persuasion into his next few movements.

He dances around on tiptoe now. He cuts the air with his big claw. In sweeping, alluring gestures he seems to describe something so exciting, he is almost irresistible. Prancing, waving, posturing, he pours out in crab-talk the most ancient message in the world. Then when he's sure he's made his point, he runs into his hole with the lady close behind him. °

Isn't love wonderful and what does this say to us about all of life?

° Dr. and Mrs. Shedd live on Fiddler's Ridge, Fripp Island, South Carolina. Fiddler's Ridge is named for the fiddler crab. Everyone living on Fiddler's Ridge has seen this dance countless times.

The Flying Squirrels

Did you know there is a squirrel that flies? Actually "glide" would be a more accurate description, but flying squirrels certainly do look like they're flying.

When they are born, baby flying squirrels weigh only three and one half ounces, and usually they come no more than two at a time.

A mature flying squirrel may grow to nine inches. It has very long feet, and between its front and hind feet is a fold of skin which looks like a spread-out wing. This is what catches the air and bears the squirrel up as it makes its way from place to place. The skin is called a "fold," because it "folds" when the squirrel is still, making the animal look like a real roly-poly.

Many people have never seen a flying squirrel, and that is because they seldom come out in daylight. They prefer the dark. Their color is slate gray with shades of brown; their underside is cream, very soft with lots of fur.

Flying squirrels usually live in trees. They seem to prefer hollow trees, but sometimes they live in people's attics or in unused fireplaces. They have very bright eyes which can see in the dark but that's not all. Their long whiskers enable them to feel their way too. Flying squirrels eat nuts and insects and, like other squirrels, they hide food for later use.

Flying squirrels often sleep head down, because their sharp claws help them hang on. They make small noises which, if amplified, would sound like a dog barking.

If you were to find a baby flying squirrel on the ground (that happens sometimes), you could make it into an excellent pet; gentle, fun, affectionate.°

° The Shedds grew up in a wooded area of the Midwest where there were many flying squirrels. Some of them became real pets. Grandchildren love stories about pets, both the ordinary and the unusual.

If we knew all there is to know about all the little creatures in our world, maybe we would know exactly what the Bible means when it says:

> *Blessed be the Lord*
> *for the precious things of the earth.*
> Deuteronomy 33:13–16

Turtle Tears

Sea turtles grow to mammoth proportions. Some of them full grown are seven feet across and they can weigh more than a thousand pounds. At this size they are so much bigger than anyone would expect, they are often called leviathan. Leviathan means "great, giant, of mammoth size." Scientists say that sea turtles lived in our world more than two hundred million years ago.

Loggerhead turtles spend all their lives in the ocean. If you have been on water much, you probably have seen the turtles, large or small, coming up for air.

When the mother loggerhead is ready to build her nest, she does an interesting thing. She comes to land, picks out a soft place in the sand, digs a deep hole, and then lays her eggs; many, many eggs; sometimes more than a hundred. If you could see her while she is about this, you would think she is crying. Great tears come from her eyes, not for sadness, but because that's how she is made. The sea turtle has eye glands which store salt and these glands can give the impression turtles really do cry.

When the mother turtle finishes laying her eggs, she goes back to sea and the eggs are left buried in the sand. After sixty days the baby turtles begin to hatch. With their strong little flippers, they push aside the sand above their nest and come to the surface. Then what do you think they do? They turn and move directly out to sea. Why don't they crawl back toward land, or to the right, or to the left? Why always toward the sea? Are they equipped with some mysterious radar?

On many islands where loggerheads come ashore to nest, nature lovers band together to protect the baby turtles. Coons, ants, and birds of prey find the eggs and destroy them. Sometimes even people, if they can, dig them up to sell. Turtle eggs are considered a delicacy, because they can be made into some very tasty things.

So the nature lovers conduct what they call "morning watch." They look for new nests. Then they mark the nesting spots and sixty days later they check to see if the babies have hatched. If there are turtle enemies around, these nature lovers may even help the baby turtles get started toward the water. But "started" is an important word, because the babies must make that long crawl *to* the water to develop strength for their survival *in* the water.

Seven years later, when a female turtle has grown to adulthood, she does another amazing thing. When she is ready to lay her eggs, she comes back where she was born to make her nest.

Did you know there is a verse in the Bible that says God made the Leviathan? And it also says, "How marvelous are thy works. In wisdom hast thou made them all."

The Pacific Golden Plover

In all thy ways acknowledge him,
and he shall direct thy paths.
                              Proverbs 3:6

Plovers are small birds with narrow pointed wings. Their flight is direct and fast. They are hatched in the northlands of Alaska. But after they are born a most unusual thing happens.

Before the young are old enough to fly great distances, the father and mother birds desert their young and fly by themselves far away to the Hawaiian Islands. So the young birds are left behind to grow strong.

Then one day when they are strong enough, these young birds rise to the sky and set their course out over the Pacific. Now they must cross two thousand miles of ocean with no ground markers to guide them. They have never made this journey before, and during the trip there will be not one single opportunity to stop for rest or food. Frequently they will encounter high winds, storms. Yet, without fail, they fly straight to those five tiny specks of land which are the Hawaiian Islands.

What do you *think?*

The Wounded Egret

We live by the ocean and one of our hobbies is watching the birds. They fish in our waters. Big birds. Little birds.

And here's a story we could hardly believe if we had only heard it. Yet since we saw it happen right out our window, what else could we do but believe?

This is what we saw:

An egret had been wounded. This was a very big egret, very white, very long neck. All day he stood there in the marsh, unable to fly. Waiting, forlorn, he simply stood there. By looking through our binoculars we could see the problem. The poor bird had a broken wing.

Egrets are not particularly kind to other egrets. If you could watch them as much as we watch them, you'd know that's true. They work a wide area and they don't like intruders, but now an amazing thing happened.

Did they have a conference and decide what they would do? Was there a meeting of the board? Or is it an unspoken rule of the egrets that birds with broken wings get special treatment?

However they decided it, the other big white birds began protecting their wounded brother. They hovered over him, brought him food, checked on him often until at last he was gone. One day when we came home from town he wasn't there.

We weren't surprised really. For several days the broken wing had been moving, then flapping with more vigor, and we'd been cheering for him.

No, we can't say we saw him fly away. But we like to think that's how he left us. And we also wish the naturalists who say that birds are always cruel had seen this drama from our window.

There is an ancient question of the philosophers, "Is the universe basically friendly?"

Good question, isn't it?

CHAPTER FOUR

Bible Stories

By some ingenious maneuvering (honest, but very clever) a financial executive we know saved his company from disaster. It was the kind of maneuver which brought all the company employees into a solution. Since many of our church members worked for his company, the man who saved their jobs was some kind of hero.

He also taught Sunday school, fifth graders. One night at a teachers' meeting, long after the crisis had passed, he told us this dream:

> "I dreamed I died and went to heaven, only I wasn't really in yet. Of course, I met St. Peter and, believe me, that wasn't all good times. He really worked me over, asked questions, brought up things I'd even forgotten, wanted to know it all. So finally it was over and he told me to wait right there. He'd have to discuss me with the committee.
>
> "I tell you for sure that was one long wait. Then he came back and all he said was, 'It was close, but they decided to let you in because you took some stories from The Book and told them to the children.' Wasn't that something?"

But one of Joseph's brothers, whose name was Reuben, intended to save him, so he said, "Do not take his life! Only throw him down into this dry well, and leave him here!" Joseph approached, and his brothers seized him and stripped off his coat. Then they threw him down into the well, and they themselves sat down to eat.

As they were finishing their meal, the brothers looked up and saw a band of Ishmaelite merchants going by with their camels laden. This gave them an idea. "Let us not do any more harm to Joseph," said his brother Judah. "After all, he is our brother, and our flesh and blood! Let us merely sell him into slavery."

So they went to find Joseph in the well, but as it happened, he had already been stolen away by another band of travelers and brought to the Ishmaelites. Reuben saw him gone and cried out in fear, "What shall we do?" The other brothers gathered together, then, plotting a way to hide their wickedness from their father, Israel. They killed a goat and smeared its blood upon Joseph's fine coat, then they sent the bloodstained garment back to their father with a message, asking him, "Is this the clothing of your son?"

"Alas, alas, it is," cried Israel. "My son is dead! He must have been torn to pieces and devoured by some wild beast, for see—here is his blood!" And Joseph's father wept, and he put on mourning clothes of sackcloth for his son, and would not be comforted. But Joseph, meantime, had been sold to the Ishmaelites for twenty pieces of silver. He was alive, a slave among camels laden with spices and resin, bound for the land of Egypt.

David and Goliath—Be Yourself

Do you ever feel as if people are trying to make you over? That's how David must have felt one day and this is the story:

David's brothers were in the army and he had come to bring them food. This must have been exciting for David. He was only a shepherd boy and now he was here for a visit to the soldiers.

But when he arrived, it wasn't at all like David thought it would be. Here they were, all these brave men, huddled together, afraid. Every day, morning and evening (sometimes oftener), a huge giant from the enemy troops came down by the river to roar and threaten.

This was the biggest man David had ever seen. His name was Goliath and he was a true giant. Then, as he studied the scene, David had

° The story of David and Goliath is found in I Samuel 17.

an idea. Could he possibly bring the giant down with one smooth stone from his sling?

All these years tending sheep, David had practiced out there on the hills. With his sling he had defended the flocks. He had killed a bear, a lion, wolves, and many smaller enemies. With all kinds of time to develop his skill, he knew he could hit even the smallest target. He was sure he could do it. Why shouldn't he deliver his people from the giant?

When David let it be known that he was willing to try, some of the soldiers took him to King Saul. "But," said the king, "you are only a mere lad. How can you go against the giant?" Yet David was so confident, and with no other options, the king gave his consent. Then he suited David in a coat of heavy armor with breastplate, helmet, sword, shield, the finest. And Saul said, "Go, and the Lord be with you."

But when David turned to walk away, he knew something was wrong. This wasn't for him. He was a shepherd, not a soldier. Clanking around in all of this, what chance would he have against the giant? "I need to be myself," he thought, and that's what he told the king.

So, laying aside the armor, David went down to the brook and selected five smooth stones. Then he turned to meet Goliath.

When the giant saw him coming, he called in derision, "Do you think I'm a dog that you send a child against me?" He called down curses on David, but David did not panic. Instead he said, "God will come to help me." Then he chose the smoothest stone, took aim, let fly, and struck Goliath in the temple.

Down like a falling tree the giant fell. David had delivered his people from their enemy. Just like he said, God really had come to help a shepherd boy determined to be himself. °

Why does it matter whether we are true to ourselves?

"I Will Water Your Camels, Too"

She didn't need to do what she did, but nice people often do the little extras.

Her name was Rebekah, and the Bible says she was selected by an old servant looking for the best. Abraham was the servant's master and Abraham was an old, old man. He had everything he wanted, with one exception. Before he died, he wanted to see his daughter-in-law.

This may sound strange, but in that day it was the custom for parents to decide who their sons and daughters would marry. So Abraham called his old servant and told him, "I want you to go where the best people live and find a wife for Isaac." Isaac was Abraham's only son and Isaac was very special. He had been born long after Abraham had given up hope of having a son.

Taking gifts for the bride's parents (that was another custom), the old servant set out. When he arrived where Abraham had told him to go, he went to the well. That was a good idea, because every day the village girls came to draw water.

What would you do first if you had an assignment like this? Before anything else the old servant prayed. He asked God to keep him alert, to guide his thoughts, to help him make the right choice.

Then he saw Rebekah. She was beautiful, and something about her made the old servant want to know more. To begin the conversation he asked her for a drink. Have you ever noticed how strangers like to help you? When you ask for directions, or if you need something, most people do try to accommodate you. That's how it was with Rebekah. Right away she took her pitcher from her shoulder and gave him water. But that isn't all.

When she had given him a drink, she said, "I will water your camels too." That may not sound like much to us. But do you know how much a camel drinks? And do you know how many camels there

were? If you will read Genesis 24, you will find the answer. You will also see this was no small offer.

As the old servant watched her, he must have thought, "Wouldn't she make a fine wife? This girl does so much more than she needs to do. She also cares about animals, and that's another good sign. I must find out who she is and where she lives. I will ask to see her parents."

That was a good idea, wasn't it? We do know people better when we have been inside their homes; when we meet their relatives.

The Bible says her family welcomed the old servant and listened as he told them why he had come. He described Isaac and then he asked if he could take Rebekah back with him. Now comes another nice moment. Her parents said, "We will call Rebekah and ask what she thinks." What would she do?

You simply must read Genesis 24. It is one of the greatest love stories ever. A truly beautiful story with many beautiful touches. And one of the most beautiful touches is the full meaning of these six words: "I will water your camels too."

Always the really beautiful people are those who think about others.

What are some little extras we could be doing to make life better for someone else?

Five Loaves and Two Small Fishes

The Bible has some nice things to say about boys and girls. And one of the nicest comes from a story called "The Feeding of the Five Thousand."

This is how it happened. In Bible times even children would go to hear a speaker. They didn't have television; there were no movies; no athletic contests in big stadiums; no circus; no computer games. There weren't many exciting things for their parents either. So this may be one reason why crowds flocked to hear a wise man speak.

At the time of our story five thousand people had come to hear Jesus. They were gathered on a hill by the lake and some scholars say Jesus spoke from a boat.

A good speaker has the ability to feel what his audience is feeling, and Jesus was especially sensitive. Right now he knew the people were hungry, so he called the disciples. When he suggested they should feed this crowd, their first reaction was, "Wherever could we find that much food, and if we could where would we get the money?" These are the things they told Jesus, but he wouldn't give up.

"Can't we find something?" he asked. Then Andrew said (Andrew seemed always to be especially alert), "There is a small boy here with five barley loaves and two small fishes." Naturally everyone was thinking, "What are these among so many?"

We do not know all the details, but one thing we do know—this small boy was glad to offer what he had. And that is what Jesus needed: a starting place. Beginning right there, he told the crowd to sit down. Then he said a prayer, and what do you think happened?

It was a miracle. The Bible says they *all* had enough to eat with twelve baskets left over.

Some of us believe Jesus knew certain things about the laws of God which we don't know. That could explain the multiplication of those loaves and fishes, couldn't it?

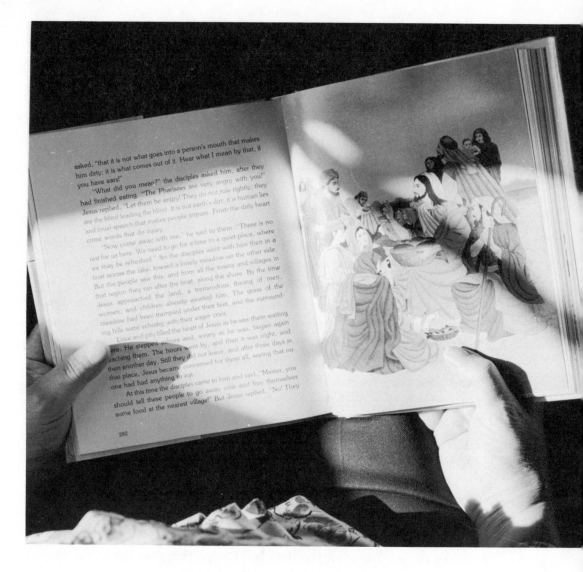

There are even scholars who say the miracle happened like this: When those five thousand people saw that one small boy offer his lunch, they reached in their robes and offered what they had, too.

What do you *think?*

The Prodigal Son

Once upon a time there was a boy who decided to leave home. We are not told exactly how old he was, but we know he was tired of working for his father. He wanted to be free. In addition, he wanted to see the world, make new friends, take in the sights.

This young man belonged to a society where he could ask in advance for his eventual share of the father's estate. So that's what he did, and off he went.

While his money lasted, he had a great time. Actually, it would be more accurate to say he had a great time for a short time, and always that's how it was. Everywhere he went the great time was only a short time. Then he would be bored, and he'd go on to another place, and another.

Finally, because he had not invested his money wisely, nor planned his future well, he ran out of funds.

Unfortunately, there came a famine in the land. Everyone was hungry, including the boy. Nothing to eat. The only job he could get was tending pigs for a farmer. That must have been a terrible comedown for a boy who had gone off to enjoy himself. Tending pigs was not exactly his idea of success.

The more he thought about all this, the more the boy realized how foolish he had been. Here he was working in a low-pay job, hungry, no future. Back there at home, even the servants had enough to eat. He knew what he would do. He would go back to his father and he would say, "I have sinned against heaven and in your sight. Make me as one of your hired servants."

Then what happened? I am glad to tell you because you are about to hear some of the most beautiful words ever written:

> While he was yet a great way off, his father saw him and his heart was filled with gladness. He ran and threw his arms around his son.

Then he kissed him and called to his servants, "Bring the best robe and put it on him. Put a ring on his finger and shoes on his feet. Come, let us celebrate with a great feast! For this my son was dead, and he is alive again; he was lost, and now he is found."

Of all the stories Jesus told, this one is everybody's favorite.° Do you suppose the reason is that all of us want to believe:

> *No matter how far we have gone,*
> *No matter what we have done,*
> *God is like a father*
> *who wants us to come home.*

° The story of the Prodigal Son is from Luke 15.

tenderly." Then he called to his servants, "Quickly! Bring my best robe and put it on my son; and put a ring on his finger and shoes on his feet. And kill the fatted calf, for we shall eat and make merry today. This is my son who was dead, and he is alive again! This is my son who was lost, and now he is found!"

CHAPTER FIVE

Poems

Almost every grandparent has a favorite poem, or many. Some of these are favorites because they came to us when we needed them. And having blessed us, they are a part of our legacy, treasures from our past.

Many grandchildren these days know very little about poetry. Or if they do know poetry, the kind they know is not our kind.

One grandfather told us he was a Longfellow buff and most of his grandchildren had never heard of Longfellow. "When I introduced them to Longfellow," he says, "they expected a basketball star!" So what did he do? He went through his Longfellow literature, selected, edited, reworked, until Longfellow came alive with interesting things for them. Then he adds, "Did they ever love *Hiawatha!*"

Some of the poems we grew up with were old when we were young. Many of these date back so far nobody knows who wrote them. That adds a certain mysterious flavor when we think it through. An ancient fellow pilgrim, far off in the distant past, comes down the long road now to bless us.

So poems, carefully selected from our treasury, may be ready made for some great times "wondering." And isn't there something about many poems so right for our two magic phrases:

"WHAT DO *YOU* THINK?"
"TELL ME MORE."

The Falling Apples

The apples falling from our tree
Make such a heavy bump at night,
I always am surprised to see
They are so little when it's light.

And all the dark just sings and sings
So loud! I cannot see at all
How frogs and crickets and such things
That make the noise can be so small.

Then my own room looks bigger too—
Corners so dark and far away!
I wonder if things really do
Grow up by night and shrink by day.

Author unknown

The Blacksmith

Last eve I paused beside the blacksmith's door
And heard the anvil ring the vesper chime.
Then looking in I saw upon the floor
Old hammers worn with beating years of time.

"How many anvils have you had," said I,
"To wear and batter all these hammers so?"
"Just one," the smith replied.
"The anvil wears the hammers out, you know."

And so I thought how like God's truth
For ages skeptic blows have beat upon
Yet still throughout the years it stands,
The anvil is unworn, the hammers gone.

Author unknown

Just the Place for Us

Dad learned high-pressure salesmanship
  And sharpened it with skill and grace.
He wrote an ad to sell our house,
  A great description of the place.

He told its charm in all detail,
  Lawn, basement, attic, shelf and drawer,
And then he turned to mom and said,
  "Just what we've been looking for!"

You Too?

When you get to heaven
You will likely view
Many folk whose presence there
Will be a shock to you.

But do not look astonished,
Do not even stare.
Doubtless there'll be many folk
Surprised to see you there.

Author unknown

Abou Ben Adhem*

ABOU BEN ADHEM *(may his tribe increase!)*
Awoke one night from a deep dream of peace,
And saw, within the moonlight in his room,
Making it rich, and like a lily in bloom,
An angel writing in a book of gold:—
Exceeding peace had made Ben Adhem bold,
And to the Presence in the room he said,
"What writest thou?"—The vision raised its head,
And with a look made of all sweet accord,
Answered, "The names of those who love the Lord."
"And is mine one?" said Abou. "Nay, not so,"
Replied the angel. Abou spoke more low,
But cheerly still; and said, "I pray thee, then,
Write me as one that loves his fellow-men."
The angel wrote, and vanished. The next night
It came again with a great wakening light,
And showed the names whom love of God had blessed,
And lo! Ben Adhem's name led all the rest.

Leigh Hunt [*1784–1859*]

* From Burton Egbert Stevenson, *The Home Book of Verse* (New York: Henry Holt and Company, 1915).

The Blind Men and the Elephant

It was six men of Indostan,
To learning much inclined,
Who went to see the elephant
(Though all of them were blind),
That each by observation
Might satisfy his mind.

The first approached the elephant,
And, happening to fall
Against his broad and sturdy side,
At once began to bawl:
"God bless me! but the elephant
Is very like a wall!"

The second, feeling of the tusk,
Cried: "Ho! what have we here,
So very round, and smooth, and sharp?
To me 'tis very clear,
This wonder of an elephant
Is very like a spear!"

The third approached the animal,
And, happening to take
The squirming trunk within his hands,
Thus boldly up he spake:
"I see," quoth he, "the elephant
Is very like a snake!"

The fourth reached out his eager hand,
And felt about the knee:
"What most this wondrous beast is like,
Is very plain," quoth he;

" 'Tis clear enough the elephant
     Is very like a tree!"

The fifth, who chanced to touch the ear,
     Said: "E'en the blindest man
Can tell what this resembles most:
     Deny the fact who can,
This marvel of an elephant
     Is very like a fan!"

The sixth no sooner had begun
     About the beast to grope
Than, seizing on the swinging tail
     That fell within his scope,
"I see," quoth he, "the elephant
     Is very like a rope!"

And so these men of Indostan
     Disputed loud and long,
Each in his own opinion
     Exceedingly stiff and strong,
Though each was partly in the right,
     And all were in the wrong!

                    John Godfrey Saxe

CHAPTER SIX

When Time Is Short

On certain occasions mini-stories may be the thing for grandpa-grandma-grand-child wondering.
  Over the phone
  on busy days
  when there are too many things for a grandchild to do
  too many things on our list, too
All these make it a fact:
  The carefully selected small item can be the very thing for the very few minutes we can share.

Choice

A great poet once asked, "What would you do if God came to you and said, 'Behold! In one hand I hold before you pure truth. In the other hand I hold the search for truth. Choose which you will have!' Which will you choose?"

Which would you *choose?*

Never

A famous philosopher was once asked, "At what period in your life did you begin to feel you had a complete grasp of your subject?"

To which the philosopher answered, "Never."

Now why would he say that?

Directions

Rufus Jones, a famous American Quaker, tells of a foot traveler who once asked a boy how far it was to a certain town. To which the boy gave him this answer: "If you go the way you are headed, sir, it will be twenty-five thousand miles. If you turn around and go in that direction, it will be about three."

Whatever could this little story mean?

The Two Buckets

Two buckets went one day to the well and, as they were going, the one frowned and said, "Isn't this a miserable life for us? Did you ever stop to think, no matter how many times we go away from this well full, we always come back empty?"

To which the other bucket replied (laughing and with happy smile), "I'd never thought of it like that. In fact, I was just thinking, isn't it fine, no matter how many times we come to this well empty, we always go away full?"

Questionnaire
1. *Can you think of some people who are like the first bucket?*
2. *And others like the second?*
3. Good question for grandparents *and* grandchildren: *Which one am I most like?*

The Worst Curse

The Tatar tribes of Central Asia had a curse they hurled against their enemies. They did not shout or swear. They only said:

"May you stay in one place forever."

Indian Chief

Once upon a time an old Indian chief, weak and fading every day, lived among the mountains near the seashore. He was unable now to roam the country he loved. But loving it as he did, he called his three grandsons and said, "You are young and I am old. I am weak, but you are strong. Someday soon I go to the happy hunting ground, and one more time before I go, I want to 'feel' the world around me. Go, each of you, to the hills now and bring back something for my soul."

The first grandson went a little way into the mountains and brought back some mountain laurel flowers. Beautiful! Grandson two went even farther into the hills and found some colorful rocks. Polished by winds and the rippling streams, they too were beautiful.

But the third grandson went to the top of the mountain and he came back empty-handed. When the old chief saw he was bearing no gift, he asked, "My son, what did you bring?" To which the young brave answered, "Nothing that you can handle, grandfather. But I brought for you one glimpse of the sea."

The old warrior was silent for a time and then he said, "Your gift is the greatest gift of all."

Cycling

Cycling is big these days and from the world of two-wheel buffs comes this report:

"On cross-country jaunts we sometimes travel at night. It actually isn't all that dangerous if we go the side roads where the traffic is light. And of course we're well equipped with reflectors. Then you might never have thought it, but at night there's another plus.

"It's easier to ride up hills at night. When it's dark, we see only a few feet in front and the limited light from our headlight leaves an impression this hill is either level, or at least it isn't steep. That gives us the feeling we can go a few more feet, and then a few more feet. So before we know it we're up the hill. The trouble in daylight is that we see the whole hill, and it looks almost impossible."

Whatever could this mean for me?

Needing Special Prayer

A well-known evangelist once wrote the mayor of a big city. In preparation for his revival he requested a list of people who were in need of special prayer.

The mayor sent a copy of the city phone directory.

What do you think he had in mind?

CHAPTER SEVEN

Proverbs

Proverbs of every kind and every nation can be one superb source for grand-parent-grandchild discussion.

Most children we know, when approached in the right spirit at right times, love proverbs.

Why?

Is it because, being short, they come with built-in protection against "on and on forever"? Or could it be that meanings here are nearer the surface; easier to comprehend; more readily remembered?

In speaking to certain audiences we learn the importance of sizing up group mood. And the same for individuals, including our grandchildren. All of us experience days not made for thinking. We have other things on our minds right now or we're tired or the room is too hot. So if that's how it is for us, that's how it may be for others we're addressing. Whenever we sense the distractions, we do well to redirect our approach. And if we do not expect our grandchildren to think when they're not ready to think, they may be even more receptive to another kind of thought. This is the thought they can think about later.

What a ready-made item the proverb is for these times!

———————————

OLD COUNTRY PROVERB:

The first time someone calls you a horse, forget it.
The second time someone calls you a horse, think about it.
If a third person calls you a horse, maybe you should go buy a saddle.

———————————

"Never spend your money before you have it."   THOMAS JEFFERSON.

Life is hard by the yard but, by the inch, life's a cinch.

"Big shots are only little shots who kept on shooting."   CHRISTOPHER MORLEY.

He who fights fire with fire ends up with ashes.

"A soft answer turneth away wrath."   PROVERBS 15:1.

ANCIENT CHINESE PROVERB:
   There are five points to the compass:
   North, East, South, West,
   And the point where I am.

"That man is richest whose pleasures are cheapest."   THOREAU.

"To avoid criticism say nothing, do nothing, be nothing."   ELBERT HUBBARD.

Don't push the river.

"Sadder than the song of an owl is the mournful phrase,
   'I told you so.'"   BYRON.

A Bird in the Hand

Sometimes we assume the old proverbs we grew up with have long ago worn themselves out. But that is not necessarily so. Our grandchildren may never have heard them.

One evening our phone rang, long distance, collect. This was Kristy, our ninth-grade granddaughter, and she had a problem.

Problem: "I wish you could help me decide something. I went over to the gym this week to watch the swimming tryouts." (Very large school with pool.)

"Well, I decided, just for kicks, I'd put my tank suit in my bag next morning and see how I could do." (Since early years she's been a top-notch swimmer.) "Now I don't want to brag but, honest, I even beat the seniors, so right away the coach asked me would I try out for the team. That's O.K., but you know how I want to play basketball. I mean I really want to play basketball.

"Only basketball isn't till three weeks from now, and even if I did make the basketball team, it's the same time as swimming. You can't do both, see? And here I am making the swimming team, but I want to play basketball. What do you think I should do?"

Comes now the moment to suppress our grandparent wisdom, at least temporarily, and ask, "What do you think?" . . . and then, "Tell me more." Anything to keep them talking, to keep them coming at their problem, turning it around, this way, that way, running it over.

Then when the whole thing has been thoroughly discussed, and only then, how now for a proverb? (After all, she is asking two of her favorite people, "What do you think?")

So what do we think? What shall we say?

Proverb, an oldie for us, unknown to her, but isn't it right on target?

"Kristy, have you ever heard this one?

"A bird in the hand
Is worth two in the bush."

Long silence! Then, "Oh, I get it! Thanks."

Thank you, Great Source of Ancient Proverbs, for the right moment and the right proverb.

P.S.
She did make the swimming team, plus she was good enough for water polo too. Very few freshmen make varsity in any sport, especially in larger high schools. Now how do you suppose grandpa and grandma felt when she called again to say she made her letter?

Love those proverbs!
Almost without exception proverbs are the products of antiquity (many very, very old), giving them the feel of authenticity. Then too, many proverbs come from other lands, introducing the young to wisdom of variant cultures. Thus proverbs, though ever so short, may be ever so long for the stretching of minds.

CHAPTER EIGHT

Epitaphs

Limericks and lines, poems and pieces from graveyards hardly seem like the stuff for grandparent-grandchild thinking. But for certain types they can become a true fun item.

Visits to old cemeteries hardly sound like good times either. Yet for a reverent kind of merriment these also may develop into a game of "Look, grandpa, what I found!" or "Grandma, you won't believe this one."

And here is another possibility. Epitaph-finding might be exactly the thing for a sharing game across those miles between us.

Several versions of this epitaph are reported from a gravestone in Maine:

Sacred to the memory of
Mr. Jared Bates
who died Aug. 6, 1800
His widow, age 24, who mourns
as one who can be comforted,
lives at 7 Elm Street this village
and possesses every qualification
for a good wife.°

She went off singing.
Read her epitaph
in Proverbs 31.

By industry and economy
he acquired a handsome fortune.
He's dead.

In a village cemetery in England there is a stone with this simple inscription:

To Thomas Cobb,
who mended shoes
in this village 40 years
to the glory of God.

°*Over Their Dead Bodies*, Brattleboro, VT: Stephen Greene Press, 1962, subtitled, *Yankee Epitaphs & History*.

And this, one of our favorites, reported often in the literature of epitaphs . . . always "source unknown"

> As you are now
> So once was I
>
> As I am now
> You soon shall be.
>
> Prepare to die
> And follow me.

"Preachy" kind of grave marker, yes. But under these lines some wag had scrawled:

> To follow you
> I'm not content
> Until I know
> Which way you went.

Engraved on tombstone in small town cemetery:

> He played
> four years
> on the
> second team.
> He never gave up.

From a grave marker in southern Scotland:

> You think I'm forgot,
> But I'm not.

III

ON MAKING TIME FOR STORYTELLING

ON MAKING TIME FOR STORYTELLING

Lament of the harried grandparent:

"Do you know how many things our grandchildren have on their agenda? But that's not all. You should see ours! When would we ever find time for storytelling?"

Fact: Nobody, but nobody, ever *finds* time for storytelling. For storytelling we only *make* time!

So how?

Out of many letters from grandparents (most in response to our book, *Then God Created Grandparents and It Was Very Good*) and from reports at our grandparents' seminars, some answers now to "How?"

Bedtime

From one of the finest grandmothers we know:

"I think if we're going to be good storytellers through the years, we need to become good bedtime storytellers early, very early. My grandchildren are almost grown, but do you know I can still say, 'Let's have a story,' and almost at once they'll drop what they're doing and come for the story. Isn't that amazing? No, maybe it isn't really. I think what happens is that, whenever they hear my invitation now, it's like turning a little switch inside and here come all those warm memories. That's why I say we need to start early, at bedtime."

Best Friends

Several grandparenting couples we know (some grandmothers alone, plus one grandfather by himself) invite their grandchildren to spend a week, ten days, two weeks alone with them every summer. From one of these couples, this report:

"We began when they were three, so you can see, by the time they finish high school, we've spent a lot of time together. How does anyone become 'best

friends'? Well, one answer is, 'By spending time together.' Anyway, we can tell you we are 'best friends' with all of our grandchildren, and isn't that nice?"

Saturday Ritual

One working grandmother has an unusual Saturday morning ritual with her grandchildren. Because she must go to her office for the check of weekly sales reports, she takes a different grandchild with her every Saturday. First they go for breakfast together, then to her office. She says, "I rescued this old typewriter the company was about to discard and I even bought a typing book so they can teach themselves if they want to. Of course, I keep plenty of paper and pencils on hand, plus some coloring books. I think it's important we help them have a good time by themselves, don't you? Anyway, I can tell you that Saturday morning with grandma is one of the big things in their lives, and in mine too."

Sunday Noon

A grandfather writes, "We have four grandchildren. Since our family goes to the same church, we've established a custom of taking the grandchildren out to eat every Sunday noon. No parents allowed. Just us and the grandchildren. There's no way I can tell you how much this means to us, and I think our grandchildren feel that way too. But it isn't just eating together. You wouldn't believe some of the discussions we have at those Sunday dinners."

One Meal Alone

Another version: the grandfather who, whenever his grandchildren and their families are visiting, takes each grandchild out for one meal alone. Breakfast, lunch, dinner, grandpa and grandchild spending time, having fun, talking, discussing, wondering together.

The Shirt Salesman

We think this statement is a classic. It comes from a young salesman, now grown to adulthood.

"Our grandfather was a shirt salesman. He traveled three states, and every summer he would take each one of his grandchildren for an entire week with him. Looking back now, I wonder if he ever got tired of it. There were seven of us and I can't remember any time any one of us ever missed a summer. I know I didn't.

"Talk about fun, I mean it was fun, and I'm sure you can guess what else. We had a reverence for gramps no words could describe. Till the day he died we'd rather talk things over with him than anyone else, anywhere in the world.

"Then there is another thing. We learned so much from our trips with him, lasting things. For example, I'm in sales too and you know how important communication is in sales. And isn't it important other places too? I think it is, because everyone in our family, everyone in our neighborhood, everyone in the company, at the church, they all come to me with their troubles or just to talk. Plus my wife and I have a great thing going in our ability to communicate. Well, all this is no accident, because getting through to people is no accident either. It's an art, and I can tell you for sure where I learned the art was all those summers with gramps."

The Cassettes

Many grandparents live too far away for regular visiting; yet, from the reports coming in, there are ways to be in contact.

As per the grandpa and grandma who make cassettes for their grandchildren. Several times each year they send out selected messages. Funny things, serious things, things they remember about their grandchildren's early years. Memories are a big thing; memories of times spent with the grandchildren; or memories of special happenings in their own lives. Poems, favorite stories, these too they include.

"Some of our grandchildren," they write, "answer every one of our cassettes with a cassette of their own. This is one of the biggest things in our lives right now and we know it's also special to every one of them."

Long Distance

There are grandparents who put money for long-distance phone calls in their budget. Each grandchild is invited to call collect at least monthly. "And do you know," writes this grandfather, "we've never had a one of them abuse the privilege."

The Amateur Author

Another grandfather writes, "I'm an amateur author. Always wanted to write, but I was too busy. So, now I'm retired, I write stories for my grandchildren. Then I make copies and send to every one of them, including the married ones.

"What do I write about? Everything. Them. Me. The world. But for some reason they can't seem ever to get enough of my war stories. Naturally, I don't give them the full load, but I do want them to know war isn't as exciting as they see it on the screen.

"Then here's another thing they like. My grandchildren are all city kids, so maybe that's why they go for my stories about growing up on the farm. You think that would be a bore? Not if I don't go on too long. Or if I pick something they can relate to, like animals maybe, or some funny neighbor, or those big threshing dinners. I think that's a part of the secret, being sure it's something they can relate to."

If you are an amateur author see "Write Your Own Story," page 68.

Rock Music

And for "relating to," how's this for grandparenting par excellence? "I think," says this grandmother, "a grandchild will talk to you more if you pay close attention to the things they like and if you learn to talk about these things.

"I will give you an example. All of my grandchildren are into rock music. Now you know that rock music wouldn't be my thing. I didn't understand it, I didn't even like it, but they did. So I went to the library and began reading about the history of rock music. Not bad, not half so bad when I began to understand the background. Then I really listened to it, and it made more sense. Today, I even like some of it.

"Naturally, I would be talking with my grandchildren about all this, and when they could see I knew some things, they started asking me questions. That inspired me to study more. I went to the music store and bought a book.

"Next my grandchildren began bringing their friends around, and we had some terrific discussions. They talked about it at school and one day their principal called to ask if I would give a talk on the history of rock. That was for the junior highers. I have a grandchild in eighth grade. Then I was invited to speak to the high school. I have two grandchildren in high school.

"I'm sure you must realize what this attention has done for me personally, and has it ever upped my standing as a grandparent. Anyway, the point I want to make is that sometimes there will be better communication between us if we respect the things they like and prepare ourselves to talk about those things."

The Big Trip at Ten

In the Shedd family one time-spending tradition is "the big trip at ten." We take each ten-year-old with us on a special vacation. Just the three of us. Denmark, Holland, Hawaii, Japan, Korea, Thailand, Philippines, Alaska. Naturally, this requires considerable preplanning, plus saving.

Frequent reaction: "That may be all right for some, but we could *never* do anything so costly." True for some. Or is it? From a grandmother at one of our workshops: "I think where our grandchildren are concerned the phrase 'Let's think about it' is almost always better than 'Never.'"

IV

PRAYER OF THE TALKATIVE GRANDPARENT

Set a watch, O Lord,
before my mouth;
keep the door of my lips.
Psalm 141:3

There is a whimsical prayer seen often in the literature of senior citizenry, and in part it's a prayer for managing that ever so human tendency to add words as we add years. This too is one of these specials from "Anon." With gratitude then to Anon we have worked out a special version for the grandparent storyteller.

Lord, keep me from becoming overtalkative,
and particularly from the fatal habit
of thinking I must say something
on every subject and every occasion.

With my vast store of wisdom
it seems a pity not to use it all,
but Thou knowest I do want
to keep the roads open
between me and my grandchildren.

And especially, Lord, do help me
to remember that my grandchildren
will be helped more
by what they tell me
than by what I tell them.

Amen.